Carrie Hall's
Sampler

FAVORITE BLOCKS
FROM A CLASSIC PATTERN COLLECTION

BY BARBARA BRACKMAN

Carrie Hall's Sampler

FAVORITE BLOCKS
FROM A CLASSIC PATTERN COLLECTION

By Barbara Brackman

Editor: Deb Rowden
Designer: Amy Robertson
Photography: Aaron T. Leimkuehler
Illustration: Lon Eric Craven
Technical Editor: Jane Miller
Production assistance: Jo Ann Groves

Published by:
Kansas City Star Books
1729 Grand Blvd.
Kansas City, Missouri, USA 64108

First edition, first printing
ISBN: 978-1-933466-83-5

Library of Congress Control Number: 2008932756

Printed in the United States of America
by Walsworth Publishing Co., Marceline, MO

To order copies, call StarInfo at (816) 234-4636
and say "Books."

About the Author

Barbara Brackman has been a quilt pattern collector since she was in college. Carrie Hall's index to patterns served as an inspiration to Barbara's more comprehensive *Encyclopedia of Pieced Quilt Patterns*, which she began in 1979. For many years, she has been the Honorary Curator of Quilts at the Spencer Museum of Art. She's published several books for Kansas City Star Books, including *Women of Design: Quilts in the Newspaper*, which has sections about Carrie Hall and Rose Kretsinger. With Carrie Hall and Rose Kretsinger, she is an honoree of the Quilters Hall of Fame.

Table of *Contents*

Introduction

When I volunteered to design a block-of-the-month pattern for the Kaw Valley Quilt Guild in the year 2000, I remembered how much I loved to leaf through Carrie Hall's index to quilt patterns. I first started making quilts in the 1960s and quickly found the book she wrote with Rose Kretsinger called *The Romance of the Patchwork Quilt in America* at the Lawrence Public Library. It was one of the very few quilt books available. Tiny black and white photographs of hundreds of blocks inspired my imagination.

I was thrilled when I later came across the exact same blocks at the Spooner Thayer Art Museum at the University of Kansas. Required to sit at the back of the Art History classroom because I whispered too much to my neighbors during slideshows of Renaissance sculpture, I noticed a drawer behind me and opened it. Now I was in more trouble as I tried looking at the blocks in the dark. I finally asked if I could come in and examine the blocks in the ten minute breaks between classes. My curiosity resulted in a life-long hobby and eventually a career as a quilt pattern expert.

Carrie Hall wrote of her ambitions to make a quilt in every pattern, but she soon realized the futility of that goal. Instead, she tried to make a block in every design, stitching about 850 that are now at the Helen F. Spencer Museum of Art at K.U. Bettina Havig, who published color photos and patterns for the blocks in her 1999 book, Carrie Hall Blocks (American Quilters Society), found that Carrie obtained patterns from about 40 friends. Carrie also indexed the publications of the time, drawing designs pictured in Ruth Finley's and Marie Webster's books, as well as collecting patterns from magazines and newspapers like the Kansas City Star.

I chose a few of my favorite blocks to draft for the guild's sampler patterns with a focus on appliqué. I asked Cherié Ralston for help in designing the set because she and Jan Patek had designed several clever sampler quilts incorporating odd-sized blocks and rectangles, an idea that gives tradition a fresh look. I used the color photos in Bettina's book for shading and color information.

In the 8 years since we included a pattern every month in the guild newsletter, several quiltmakers have finished the project. We present their color ideas throughout the book.

Above: Carrie Hall's Sampler by Saundy Milroy, Lawrence, Kansas, 2007. Quilted by Lori Kukuk. Saundy was inspired to try hand appliqué by the block of the month design and tried various techniques in her carry-along handwork for three or four years. She enjoyed it so much she's decided she prefers appliqué to piecing.

Carrie Hall's Story

Carrie Hall is remembered today as author of the first comprehensive index to quilt patterns, *The Romance of the Patchwork Quilt in America*. Primarily a collector rather than an originator of quilt patterns, she had a trait important in collecting—she was a great organizer. She was also an excellent seamstress. This combination of attributes inspired her to make a quilt block in every pattern she could find, to organize these blocks in a logical fashion, and to publish the index in *Romance*— giving people who love quilts a tool for which they have been grateful since its publication in 1935.

Born in Wisconsin after the Civil War, she grew up in pioneer Kansas where she obtained an education on her own. In a 1909 letter Carrie recalled that "while other children were at their games I was to be found huddled up in a high chair near the window or under the study lamp with a book.... Books and magazines were few and far between and yet somehow I seemed always to have something interesting to read for I can remember my mother's many, many calls, 'Carrie, put that book away and come help me' ...for I was a bookworm if ever there was one."

She showed early talent for needlework, describing a Lemoyne Star quilt she pieced at seven, which "proved to be a masterpiece that was a nine-day wonder in the neighbor-

hood" and later won first prize at the county fair. "Life has brought me no honor to equal that one." The quilt blocks Carrie created 50 years later show evidence of her skill. Every pieced block is expertly machine sewn, even the most complex curves. The appliqué blocks boast beautiful hand stitching.

At age 23, Carrie moved to Leavenworth, Kansas, to become a dressmaker. The river port and railroad center was home to an army post where the Command and General Staff College had recently been established. Officers and their well-dressed ladies came to Fort Leavenworth for an extended stay in the city. Carrie's success at catering to Leavenworth's taste by copying Paris fashion is reflected in her early-20th-Century reputation as one of the most fashionable modistes in a town supporting 88 competing dressmakers.

Carrie Hackett married twice. In 1904 her first husband, Will Patterson, died at age 28 from Bright's disease, a degenerative kidney ailment, leaving Carrie a widow at age 37. In 1906, she married 41-year-old John Hall, a mechanic, and began using the name Madam Hall in her professional life.

Above: Young Carrie Hall. Photo courtesy of the Kansas State Historical Society, Topeka. Right: A selection of Carrie Hall's scrapbooks. Photo courtesy of the Kansas State Historical Society, Topeka.

Left: Carrie Hall in a 'colonial costume' she made to wear for her 'quilt talks.' Photo by Mary Ellen Everhard, Leavenworth, Kansas, about 1930.

Right: My Carrie Hall Sampler by Deb Rowden, Lawrence, Kansas, 2002. Quilted by Lori Kukuk. When Deb began quilting, she was quite sure she would never attain the skills to make an appliqué quilt. This one felt like a true victory for her.

magnitude of the undertaking." She stopped at 1,000 blocks, of which approximately 800 are now in the collection of the Spencer Museum at the University of Kansas.

In the late 1930s and early '40s, Carrie's reputation in Leavenworth toppled due to numerous circumstances. Her house was damaged in a fire, compounding financial troubles caused by her husband's declining health and book publishing costs (she had also subsidized a fashion history). A 1982 article in the *Leavenworth Times* politely refers to subsequent events. Carrie was accused of embezzlement.

> *"Madam Hall, treasurer for the Leavenworth Young Women's Christian Association, was thought to have confused organization and personal funds rather than having stooped to outright misappropriation of monies to finance her book."*

During her dressmaking years, Carrie made time for many other interests. She was an active club woman, a poet, and (pursuing a childhood dream of owning a library) she became a collector of rare books, specializing in literature on Abraham Lincoln. She characterized book collecting as her chief recreation. There was never any "...question of where to buy books. Only how can I make my book allowance cover all the books I desire—Shall I wear my last season's hat and buy another book?"

Carrie began a new hobby after World War I, sewing quilts as "pick-up work" and making a "Baker's Dozen" in the years of the quilt revival in the 1920s and '30s. While published patterns multiplied, she decided with true collector's zeal to make a block of every known pattern, writing later that she little realized "the

In the early 1980s, I interviewed several women in Leavenworth who had known Carrie. Most recalled that indeed she did stoop to outright misappropriation. She had long had difficulty handling money, spending impulsively on her collections, gambling on the stock market and horse races. She borrowed money from her friends and from the accounts of several clubs of which she was treasurer. To make up the losses, Carrie was forced to sell her house and collections. She left Leavenworth for Idaho and eventually North Platte, Nebraska, where she began another career as a dollmaker at age 75. With the same attention to detail shown in her dressmaking and quiltmaking careers, she created character dolls that enjoyed a national reputation. She died in North Platte in 1955 at the age of 88, leaving memories of a remarkable woman. — *Barbara Brackman*

A Blooming Friendship by Gabriela N. Lemmons, Tonganoxie, Kansas, 2005. Quilted by Rosie Mayhew. Gabriela used fat quarter cuts for everything but the border in this quilt made for her friend, Paula Acree.

Carrie Hall's Sampler by Georgann Eglinski, Lawrence, Kansas, 2001. Quilted by Shirley Greenhoe. Impatient for the next block of the month, Georgann started drawing her own and set the 20" blocks together with a block called Rocky Glen or the Lost Ship.

ASSEMBLY DIAGRAM

Carrie Hall's Sampler is assembled with square and rectangular pieced and appliquéd blocks.

Oakleaf & Cherries **1**	White Cloud **7** / Mexican Rose **6**	Pomegranite **9**
Currants **3**		**7**
Sadie's Choice Rose **2**	Cottage Tulips **5**	Leavenworth 9-Patch / Whig Rose **10**
Rose of LeMoyne **3**	Shadows **7**	Rose of Sharon **11**
Topeka Rose **4**	Pride of the Forest **8**	Tonganoxie 9-Patch **7** / Sadie's Choice Rose **2**

Opposite: Carrie Hall Falls for Hand-dyeds by Nan Doljac, Lawrence, Kansas, 2000-2006. Nan's sampler is a friendship quilt in the sense that she got ideas and help from her friends. The inspiration was cottons hand-dyed by Susan Fangman, Jeanne Welch suggested the scalloped border and Arlene Lawson did the tricky binding.

Carrie Hall's Sampler

DESIGNED BY BARBARA BRACKMAN
75" X 85" ✳ INCLUDES 5" OUTER BORDER

FABRIC REQUIREMENTS

Carrie liked a plain white background and traditional red, pink, green, blue and gold for her appliqué. Her pieced blocks tended to be 1930s prints.

BLOCKS

Refer to the individual block patterns for fabric needed. We supply some color suggestions but encourage you to choose your own colors for the appliqué pieces. See quilts throughout the book for color inspiration.

BACKGROUND

If you want all your background fabric to match in the whole sampler and the pieced border, buy 5 3/4 yards.

If you'd rather mix and match the sampler block backgrounds, buy:

✳ 3/4 yard each of 8 prints for the appliqué blocks and pieced border.
✳ You'll probably want one or two common fabrics in the blocks and strips, so buy 2 yards each of 2 prints. Fill in the rest with scraps.

THE APPLIQUÉ

Complete the appliqué using your favorite method. Excellent appliqué instruction is provided in Kathy Delaney's Kansas City Star book, *Hearts and Flowers: Hand Appliqué from Start to Finish.* All the patterns are drawn without seam allowances included, add them if necessary for your preferred method of appliqué.

REFERENCE

Throughout the book, we provide references to the original blocks in *The Romance of the Patchwork Quilt in America,* by Carrie A. Hall and Rose G. Kretsinger, 1935.

Oak Leaf and Cherries

PATTERN 1 * 20" FINISHED BLOCK

Carrie Hall pictured this block twice, calling it Oakleaf and Cherries on one page and Oakleaf and Currants on another (see pages 118 and 195 in *Romance*).

Quilt historian Joyce Gross found the antique quilt in California that inspired Carrie's pattern. It was made before an 1861 wedding and is one of a pair.

HOW TO MAKE THIS BLOCK

Add seams to the pattern pieces and appliqué onto a 20 1/2" square background. The leaves and central reel are one piece. Cut an 18 1/2" square of fabric and fold and press it into quarters. Trace the pattern onto the top and cut out the design in snowflake fashion. Add the 12 cherries last.

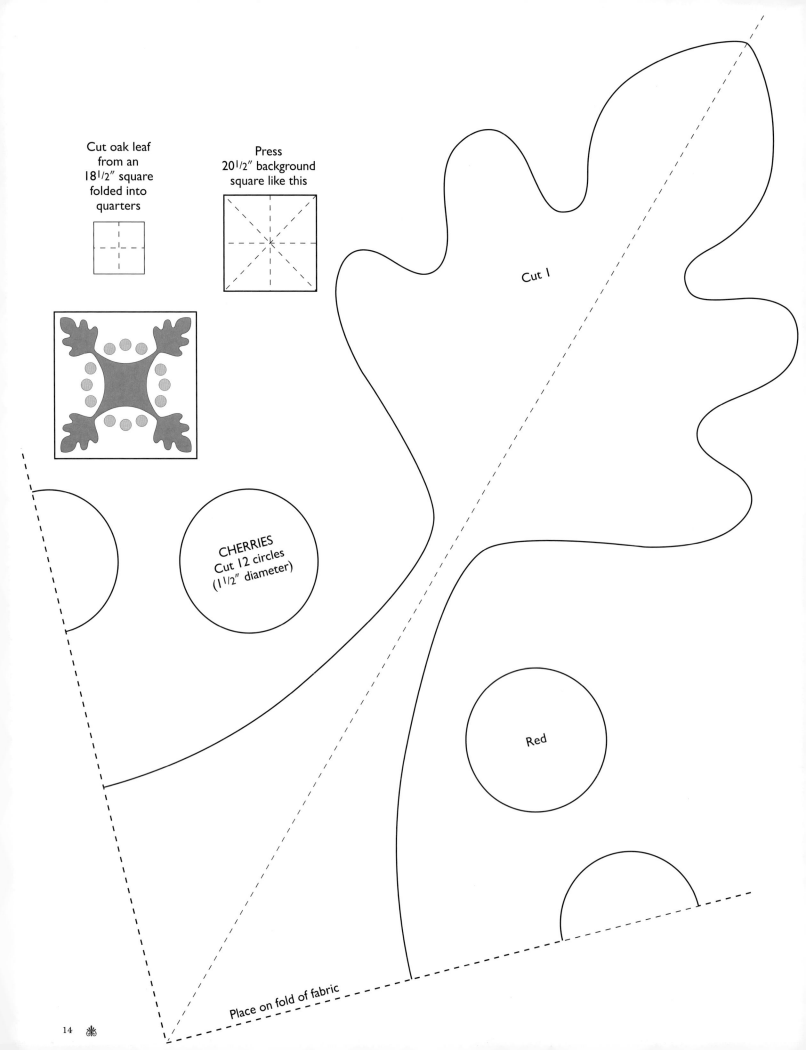

Cut oak leaf from an 18¹/₂″ square folded into quarters

Press 20¹/₂″ background square like this

Cut 1

CHERRIES
Cut 12 circles
(1¹/₂″ diameter)

Red

Place on fold of fabric

Sadie's Choice Rose

PATTERN 2 ∗ 20" FINISHED BLOCK

Notice the star that appears in the negative space around the inner circle in this design that Carrie Hall called a "very old pattern" (see page 110 in *Romance*). Newspaper pattern columnists in the 1930s called similar designs Sadie's Choice, Mexican Tea Rose and Balm of Gilead.

HOW TO MAKE THIS BLOCK
THE BUD

To fill in the spaces between the different sized blocks, make rectangular setting strips. Use this bud and stem and appliqué a 5" x 20" finished rectangle. Follow the instructions on the patterns for cutting. Cut a strip of 1/2" bias 13" long. Arrange all the pieces as shown in the photo and appliqué. Save this block to add later: it will go at the bottom right corner of the quilt.

SADIE'S CHOICE ROSE

Follow the instructions on the patterns for cutting. Add seams to the pattern pieces if necessary and appliqué onto a 20 1/2" square background.

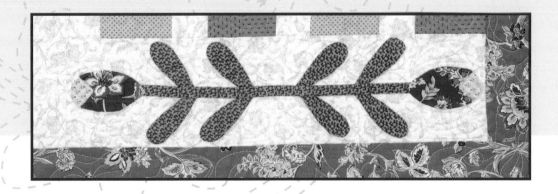

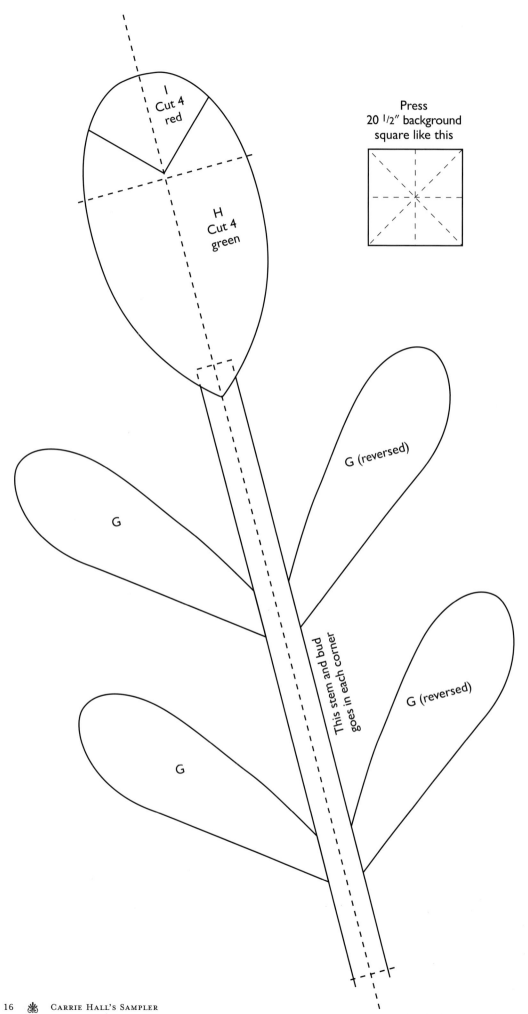

I
Cut 4
red

H
Cut 4
green

G (reversed)

G

This stem and bud goes in each corner

G

G (reversed)

Press
20 1/2" background
square like this

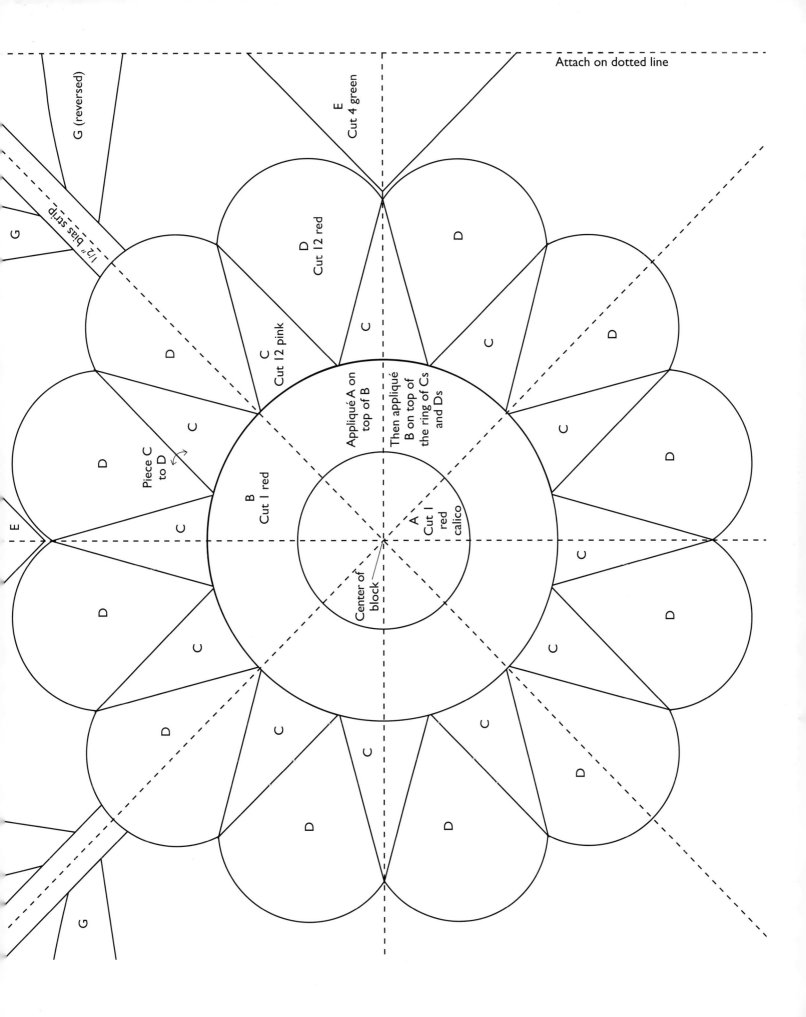

Attach on dotted line

G (reversed)

E
Cut 4 green

G

1/2" bias strip

G

D
Cut 12 red

C
Cut 12 pink

Appliqué A on top of B

Then appliqué B on top of the ring of Cs and Ds

D

C

Piece C to D

B
Cut 1 red

A
Cut 1 red calico

E

Center of block

D

C

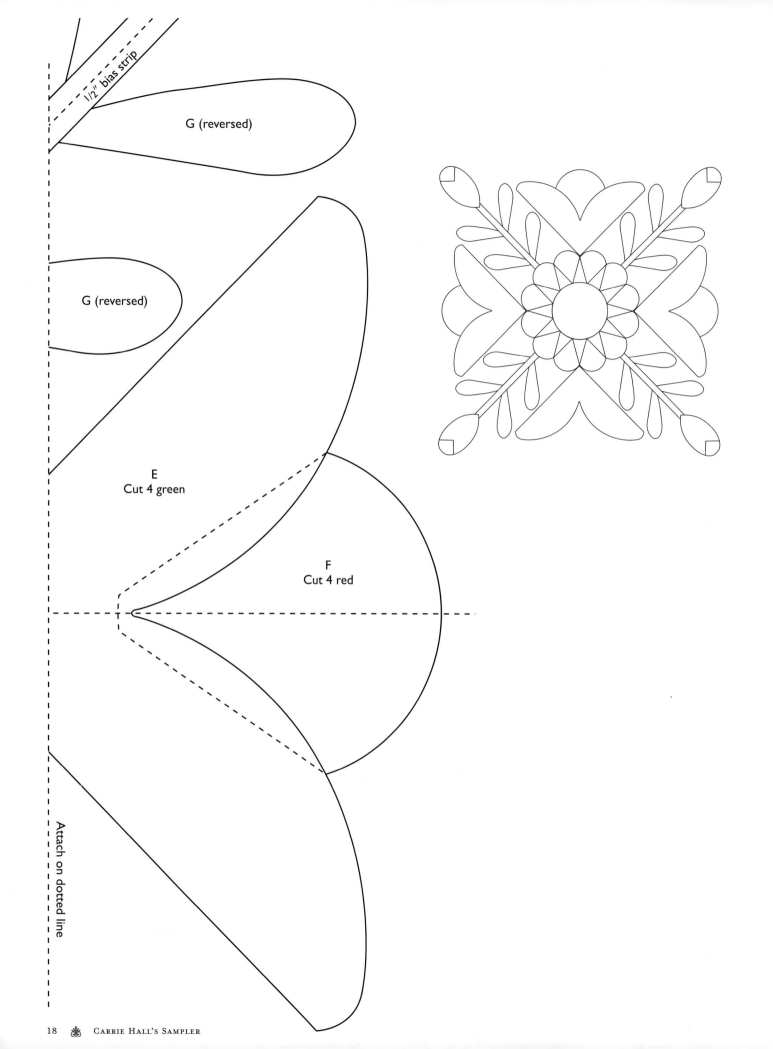

½" bias strip

G (reversed)

G (reversed)

E
Cut 4 green

F
Cut 4 red

Attach on dotted line

Rose of Lemoyne

PATTERN 3: TWO APPLIQUÉ DESIGNS TO FIT IN
THE SETTING STRIPS ✳ 10" X 20" RECTANGLE

The Rose of Lemoyne is sometimes called Love Apple
(see page 114 in *Romance*).

HOW TO MAKE THIS BLOCK

Cut a strip of background fabric 10 1/2" x 20 1/2".
The traditional pomegranate design fits in a wide rectangle,
although Hall showed it in a square on the diagonal. Follow the
instructions on the patterns for cutting.

Currants from Currants and Cockscombs

5" X 20" RECTANGLE

The strip of currants from Cockscombs and Currants (see page
120 in *Romance*) makes a skinny setting strip.

HOW TO MAKE THIS BLOCK

Cut a strip of background 5 1/2" x 20 1/2" for the currants.
Follow the instructions on the patterns for cutting.

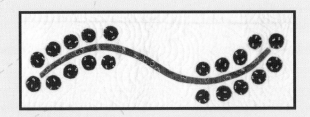

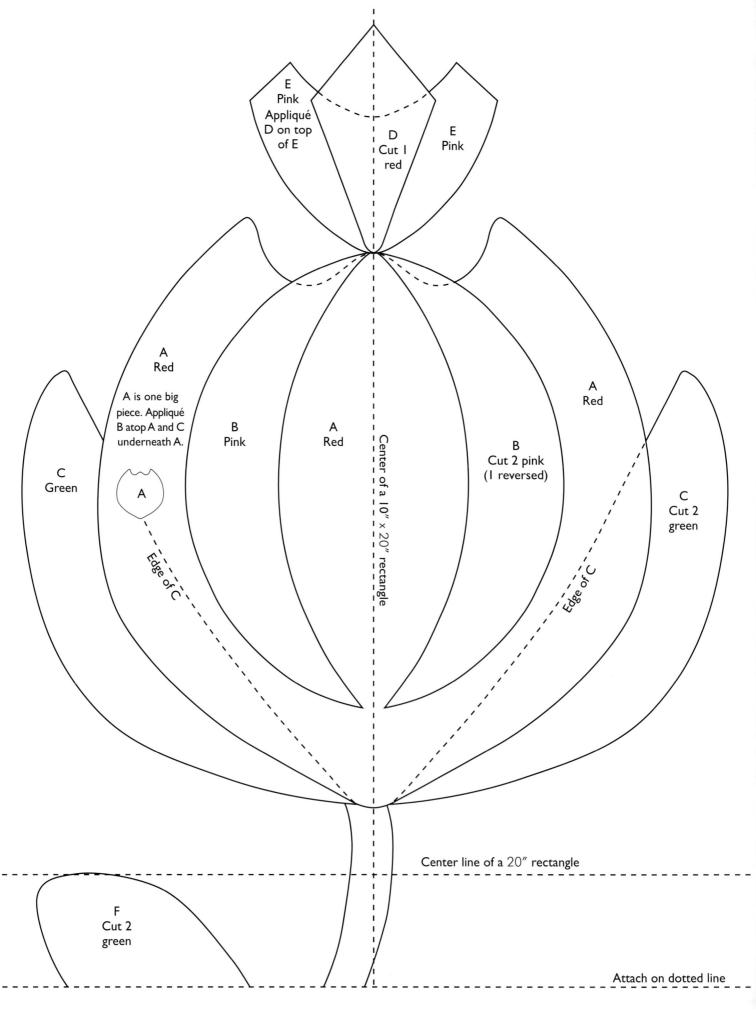

E
Pink
Appliqué
D on top
of E

D
Cut 1
red

E
Pink

A
Red

A is one big
piece. Appliqué
B atop A and C
underneath A.

C
Green

B
Pink

A
Red

A

Edge of C

Center of a 10" × 20" rectangle

A
Red

B
Cut 2 pink
(1 reversed)

C
Cut 2
green

Edge of C

Center line of a 20" rectangle

F
Cut 2
green

Attach on dotted line

Unfinished rectangle
20¹/₂"x 10¹/₂"

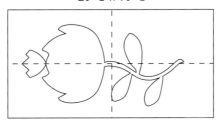

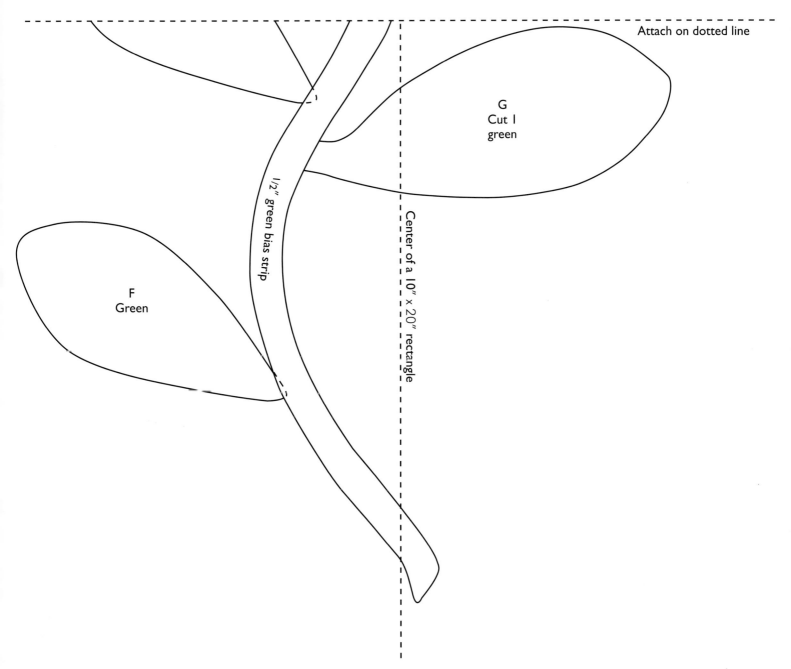

Attach on dotted line

G
Cut 1
green

F
Green

1/2" green bias strip

Center of a 10" x 20" rectangle

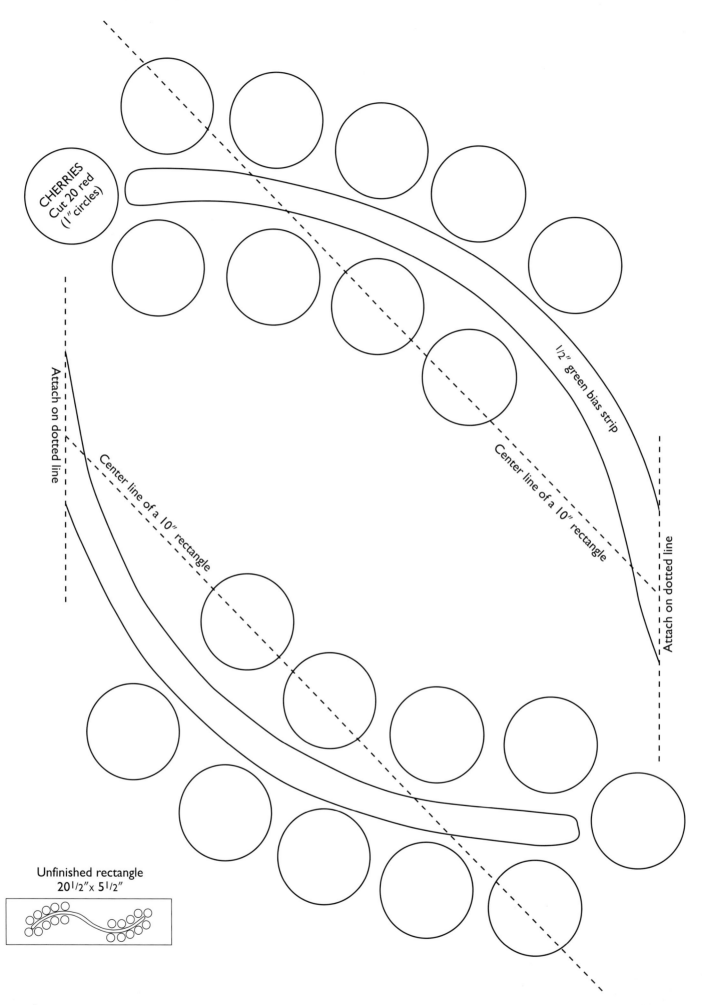

CHERRIES
Cut 20 red
(1" circles)

½" green bias strip

Attach on dotted line

Center line of a 10" rectangle

Center line of a 10" rectangle

Attach on dotted line

Center line of a 10" rectangle

Unfinished rectangle
20½" x 5½"

Topeka Rose

PATTERN 4 * 20" FINISHED BLOCK

This block, a Carrie Hall original, finishes out the left side of the quilt. During the early 1930s she drove around Kansas, giving lectures illustrated by her quilt blocks. She wore a "colonial costume" and talked about the stories behind the quilt pattern names. She named this block for the Business and Professional Women's Club of Topeka, Kansas, an organization in which she was very active. (See page 110 of *Romance.*)

Once you finish this block, you'll have the left side of the quilt finished.

HOW TO MAKE THIS BLOCK
Add seams to the pattern pieces and appliqué onto a 20 1/2" square background. The center flower is appliquéd in layers. Follow the instructions on the patterns for cutting.

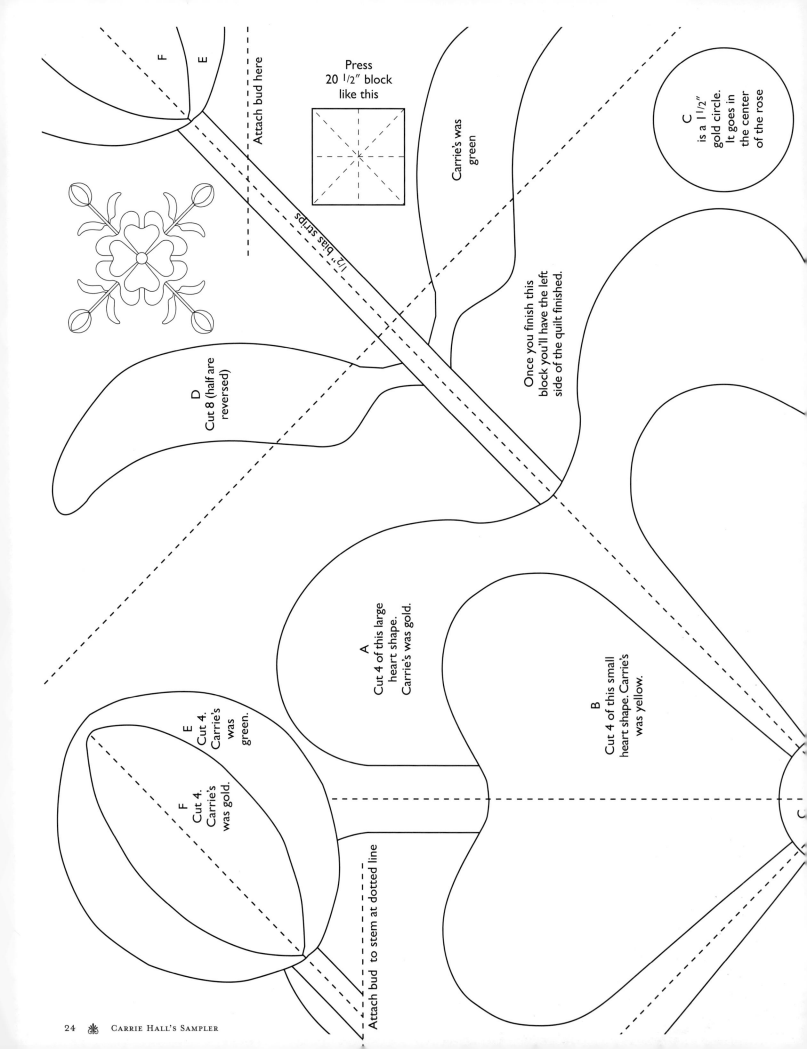

F

E

Attach bud here

Press
20 1/2" block
like this

Carrie's was
green

C
is a 1 1/2"
gold circle.
It goes in
the center
of the rose

1/2" bias strips

D
Cut 8 (half are
reversed)

Once you finish this
block you'll have the left
side of the quilt finished.

A
Cut 4 of this large
heart shape.
Carrie's was gold.

B
Cut 4 of this small
heart shape. Carrie's
was yellow.

E
Cut 4.
Carrie's
was
green.

F
Cut 4.
Carrie's
was gold.

Attach bud to stem at dotted line

C

Cottage Tulips

PATTERN 5 * 25" X 25" FINISHED BLOCK

Cottage Tulips was designed by the Kansas City Star's quilt artist Eveline Foland (see page 122 of *Romance*).

HOW TO MAKE THIS BLOCK

This block can be pieced or appliquéd onto a 25 1/2" x 25 1/2" square for the center block in your sampler. Refer to the Block Assembly Diagram on page 26 to put it together.

BLOCK ASSEMBLY DIAGRAM

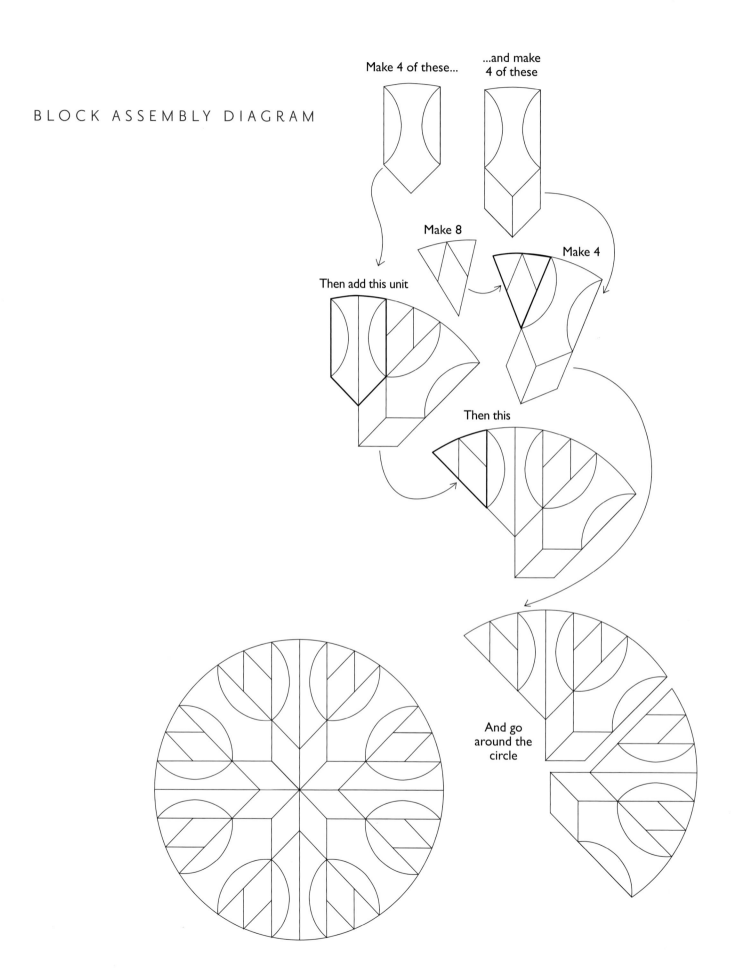

Make 4 of these...

...and make 4 of these

Make 8

Make 4

Then add this unit

Then this

And go around the circle

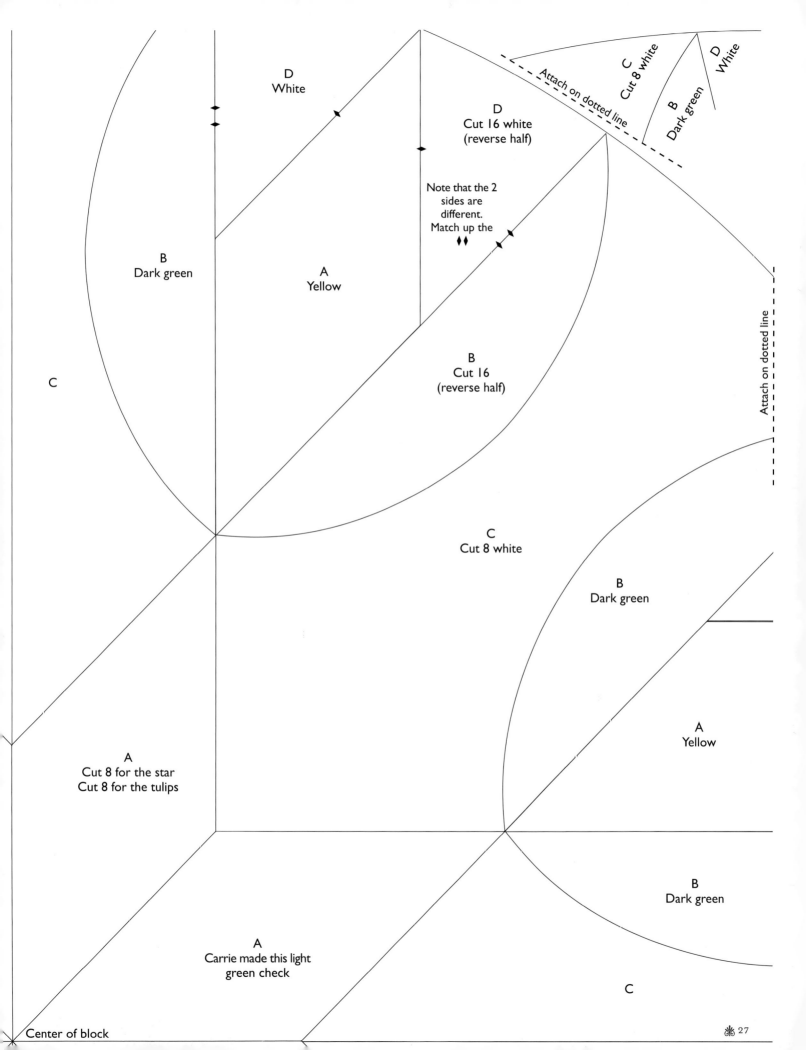

D
White

D
Cut 16 white
(reverse half)

C
Cut 8 white

B
Dark green

A
Yellow

Note that the 2
sides are
different.
Match up the

B
Cut 16
(reverse half)

C

B
Dark green

A
Yellow

Attach on dotted line

C
Cut 8 white

B
Dark green

D
White

Attach on dotted line

C
Cut 8 white

B
Dark green

A
Yellow

A
Cut 8 for the star
Cut 8 for the tulips

A
Carrie made this light
green check

C

Center of block

❋ 27

Mexican Rose

PATTERN 6 * 20" FINISHED BLOCK

Carrie Hall found this block pictured in Marie Webster's 1915 book *Quilts: Their Story and How to Make Them*. Webster noted the pattern name reflected "domestic interest in important events." The Mexican War of 1846-1848 was America's first foreign war, the conflict in which we wrested land in Texas, California, New Mexico, Arizona and southwest Kansas from Mexico. This Mexican Rose, quite popular in the late 1840s and '50s, seems an expression of politics and patriotism in quilt patterns.

HOW TO MAKE THIS BLOCK

This pattern is appliquéd onto a 20 1/2" square background. Follow the instructions on the patterns for cutting. This is a good beginning appliqué design. Note the option for cutting the flower petals as all one piece.

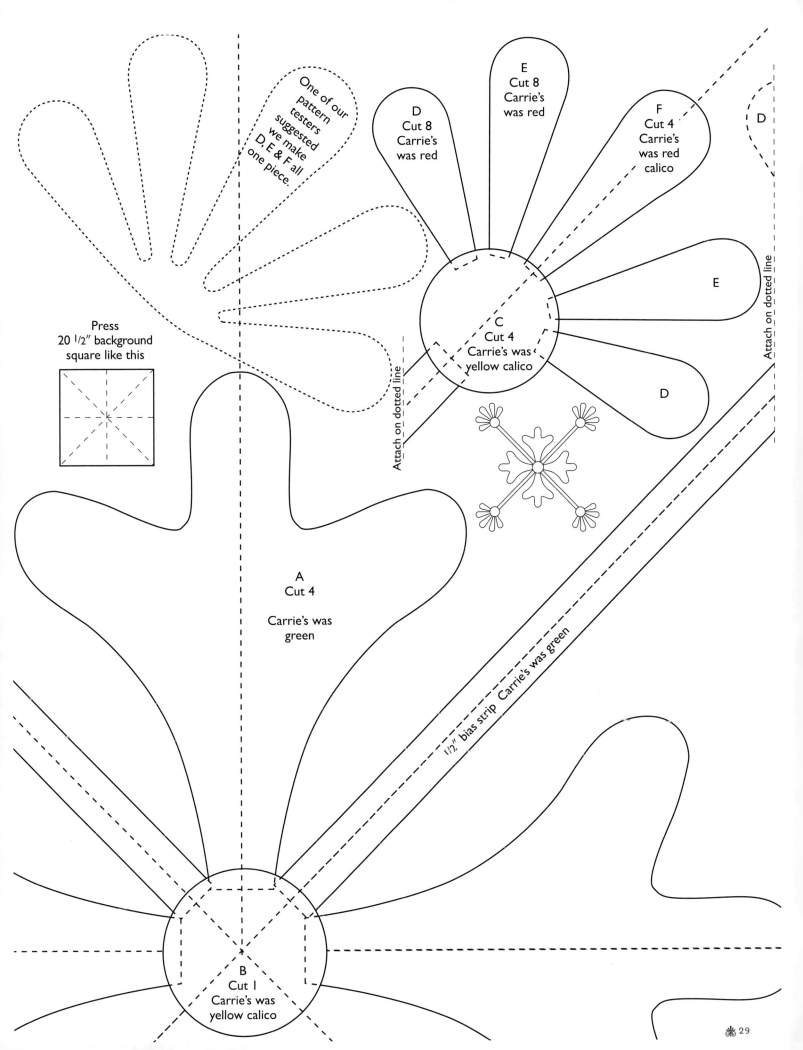

One of our pattern testers suggested we make D, E & F all one piece.

D
Cut 8
Carrie's was red

E
Cut 8
Carrie's was red

F
Cut 4
Carrie's was red calico

D

E

D

C
Cut 4
Carrie's was yellow calico

Attach on dotted line

Attach on dotted line

Press
20 1/2" background square like this

A
Cut 4

Carrie's was green

1/2" bias strip Carrie's was green

B
Cut 1
Carrie's was yellow calico

❋ 29

PATTERN 7 ✳ FOUR PIECED 5" SETTING STRIPS

The updated look of a sampler of different-size blocks requires strips to even out the geometry. Here are 4 pieced strips of blocks adapted from Carrie Hall's designs. All the blocks are 5" square when finished.

Tonganoxie Nine Patch

20" X 5" FINISHED STRIP OF 4 BLOCKS

Carrie designed a block of squares and rectangles for the Ladies' Association of the Congregational Church of Tonganoxie. She must have spoken to their group about quilt patterns. The simple nine patch here is drawn from the corner of that block. She shaded the squares to give a transparent illusion as if two light squares overlap and form a darker middle square. Make 4 blocks and put this strip between the Rose of Sharon (pattern 11, page 43) and the buds from Sadie's Choice Rose (pattern 2, page 15) in the lower right hand corner of the quilt.

ROTARY CUTTING INSTRUCTIONS
CUT 2 1/8" SQUARES:
✳ 8 of background fabric
✳ 4 of dark fabric
✳ 6 each of 4 different medium prints

Note: Slight adjustments may be needed to make these sections fit.

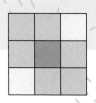
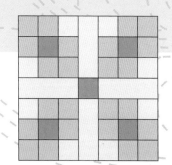

Leavenworth Nine Patch

25" X 5" FINISHED STRIP OF 5 BLOCKS

Carrie named this double nine patch for her hometown.
The 5" finished block is drawn from the corner of her original
design. Make 5 blocks into a strip to go on the left side of the
Whig Rose (pattern 10, page 41).

ROTARY cutting instructions
Cut 2 1/8" squares:
* 10 of background fabric
* 5 of another light fabric
* 30 of dark fabric

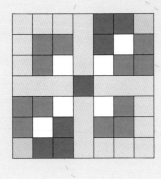

White Cloud

20" X 5" FINISHED STRIP OF 4 BLOCKS

Bettina Havig found this block, which is not pictured in Carrie's book, in the Hall collection at the Spencer Museum with the name White Cloud, possibly named for the town in the north-eastern corner of Kansas. It's an old block usually called Birds in the Air. Make four blocks into a strip for the left side of the Mexican Rose block (pattern 6, page 28).

ROTARY CUTTING INSTRUCTIONS
FOR THE LARGE TRIANGLES:

✳ Cut 2 squares 5 7/8" of medium fabric. Cut each into 2 triangles with a diagonal cut. You need 4 triangles.

FOR THE SMALL TRIANGLES:

✳ Cut 6 squares 2 1/2" of dark fabric and 12 of background fabric. Cut each into 2 triangles with a diagonal cut. You need 12 dark triangles and 24 of the background fabric.

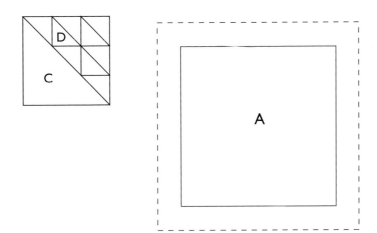

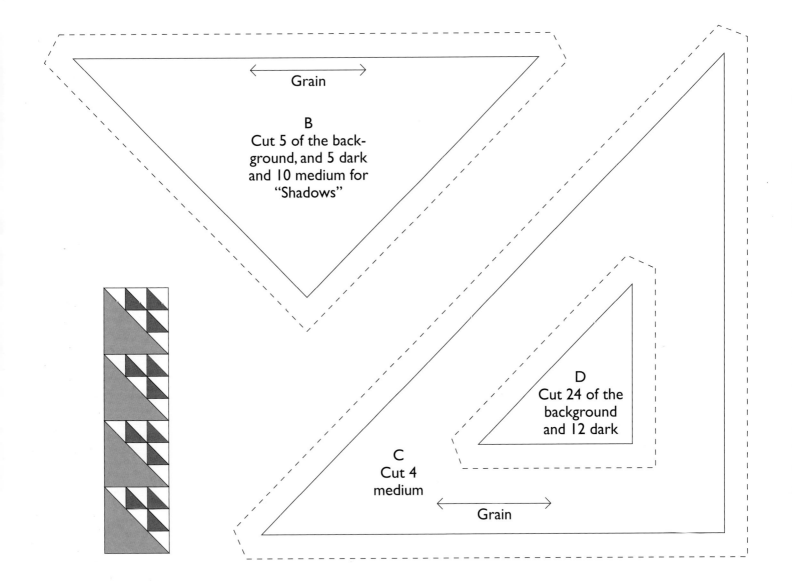

B
Cut 5 of the back-
ground, and 5 dark
and 10 medium for
"Shadows"

Grain

D
Cut 24 of the
background
and 12 dark

C
Cut 4
medium

Grain

A

Shadows

25" X 5" FINISHED STRIP OF 5 BLOCKS

Shadows is another block in the Hall collection that didn't appear in Carrie's book. It's a different shading of the old triangle design called Broken Dishes or Hour Glass. Make 5 blocks into a strip that goes below Cottage Tulips (pattern 5, page 25).

ROTARY CUTTING

❊ Cut 2 squares 6 1/4" of background fabric. Cut each into 4 triangles with 2 diagonal cuts. You need 5 triangles.

❊ Cut 3 squares 6 1/4" of medium fabric. Cut each into 4 triangles with 2 diagonal cuts. You need 10 triangles.

❊ Cut 2 squares 6 1/4" of dark fabric. Cut each into 4 triangles with 2 diagonal cuts. You need 5 triangles.

Pride of the Forest

PATTERN 8 * 25" X 25" FINISHED BLOCK

Carrie copied this design from a tiny photo in Ruth Finley's 1929 book *Old Patchwork Quilts and the Women Who Made Them* (plate 92). Finley dated the rather unusual quilt of "home-dyed Turkey red and green" to 1827. She didn't know as much about quilts as we do. The red and green appliqué quilts usually date after 1840. And Turkey red cotton was never home-dyed. It was imported as cloth from Europe. Finley interpreted the central shape as a pine tree, the feathers on each side as Boston ferns, and the corner shapes as oak leaves and acorns.

Once you've finished the Pride of the Forest block, you can piece the central strip together.

HOW TO MAKE THIS BLOCK

This is one of the two larger blocks so cut your background 25 1/2" square. Follow the instructions on the patterns for cutting. Press the background as shown and place the corner designs on the diagonal folds, close to the edges of the block.

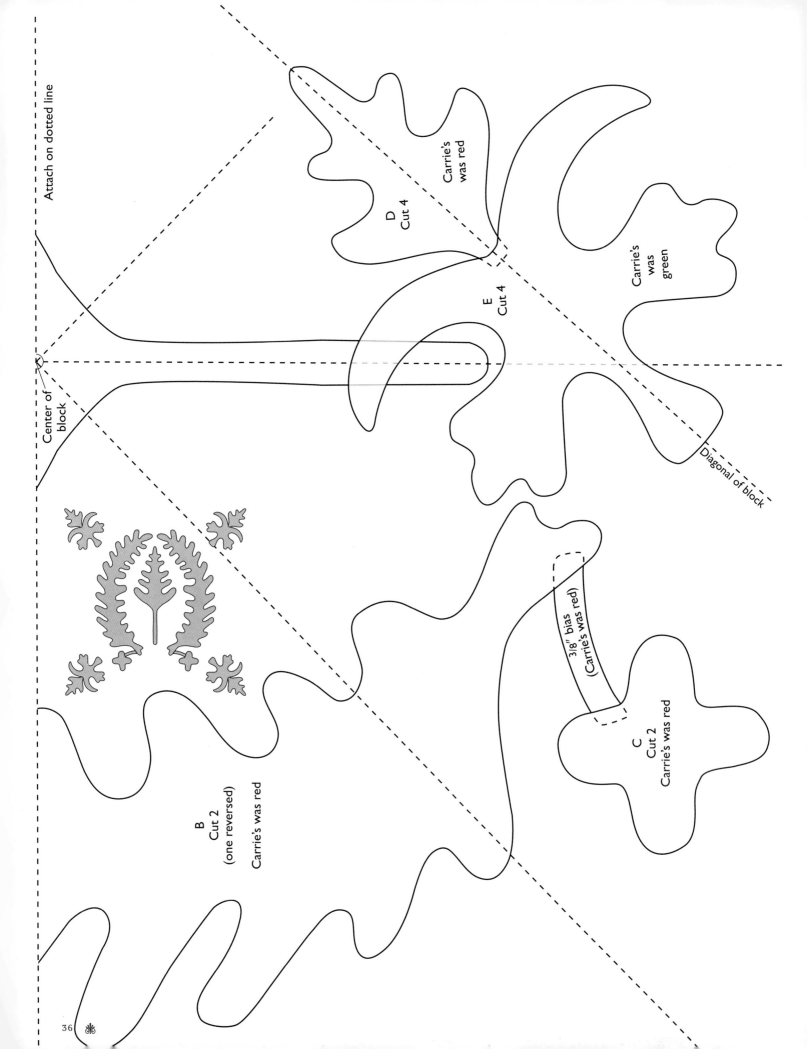

Attach on dotted line

Center of block

D
Cut 4

Carrie's was red

E
Cut 4

Carrie's was green

Diagonal of block

3/8" bias
(Carrie's was red)

C
Cut 2
Carrie's was red

B
Cut 2
(one reversed)
Carrie's was red

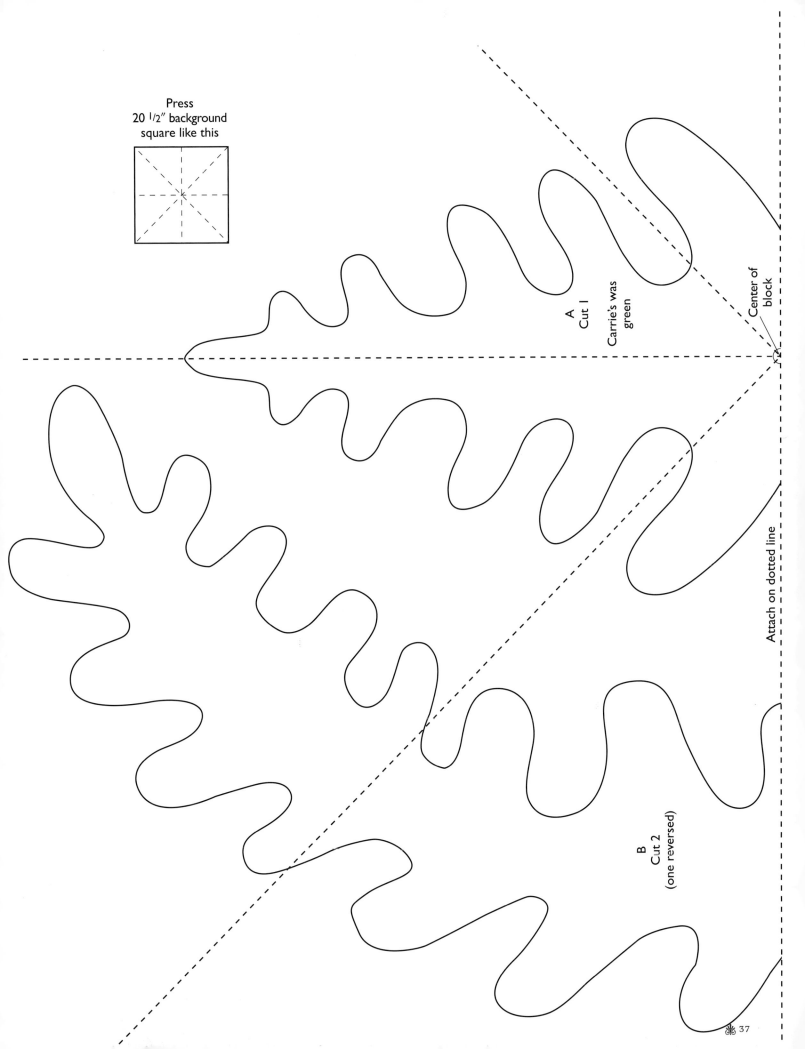

Press
20 ¹/₂" background
square like this

A
Cut 1

Carrie's was
green

Center of
block

Attach on dotted line

B
Cut 2
(one reversed)

Pomegranate

PATTERN 9 * 20" X 20" FINISHED BLOCK

Pomegranates have rich symbolism in many cultures. In Jewish metaphor, the fruit is considered to have 613 seeds corresponding to the Torah's 613 commandments. The Muslim Koran mentions it as a gift from Allah. Christian symbolism suggests it as the forbidden fruit in the Garden of Eden (a possible reason for the quilt pattern name Love Apple). It was also a forbidden fruit in Greek myth where Persephone brought about winter's curse by eating its seeds.

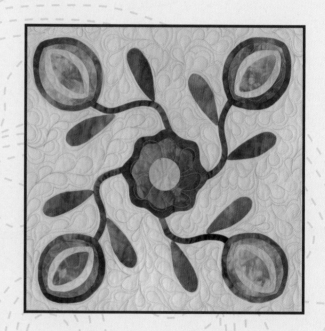

English embroiderers borrowing fanciful images from India, China and the Muslim world decorated textiles with pomegranates in their Jacobean-style crewel work. Spanish conquistadors brought the image of La Granada to New Spain where we still see it in the Navajo squash blossom.

See pattern #3 for another version of the Love Apple or pomegranate and page 11 of *Romance* for this block, which Carrie probably found in a catalog from the Ladies Art Company, a St. Louis pattern source that was among the first to sell quilt patterns through the mail. *Farm and Fireside* magazine also published it under the name Rose and Peony in 1929.

HOW TO MAKE THIS BLOCK

This pattern is appliquéd onto a 20 1/2" square background. Follow the instructions on the patterns for cutting. Press the background as shown in the diagram and arrange the pieces as shown in the photo.

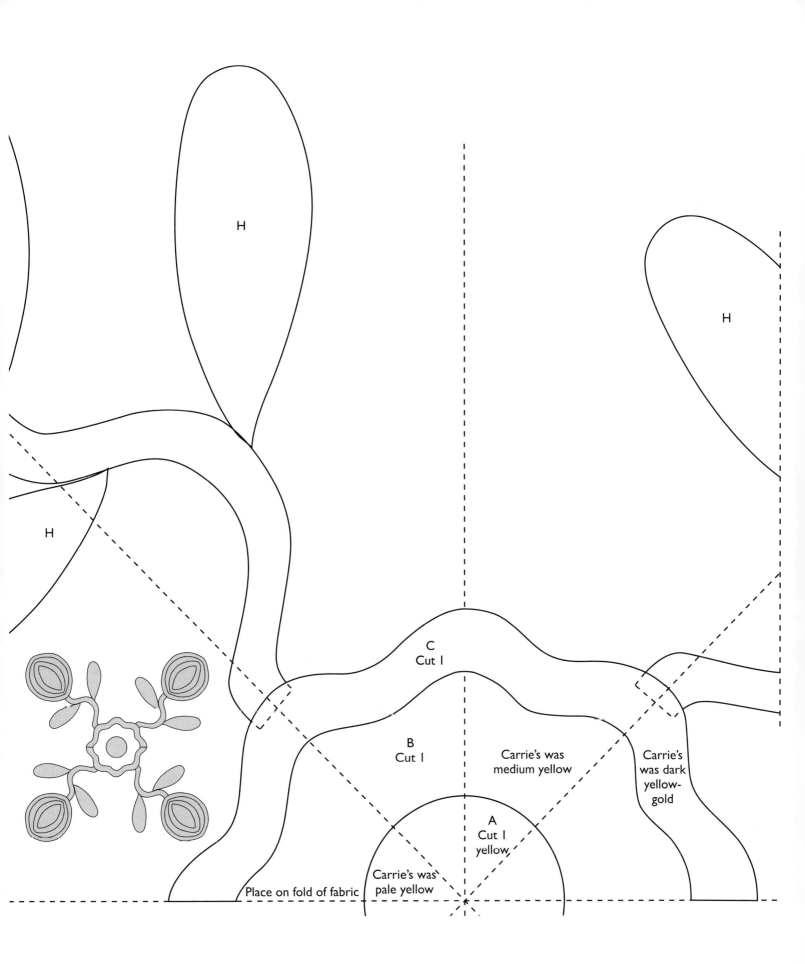

H

H

H

H

C
Cut 1

B
Cut 1

Carrie's was
medium yellow

Carrie's was dark
yellow-
gold

A
Cut 1
yellow

Place on fold of fabric

Carrie's was
pale yellow

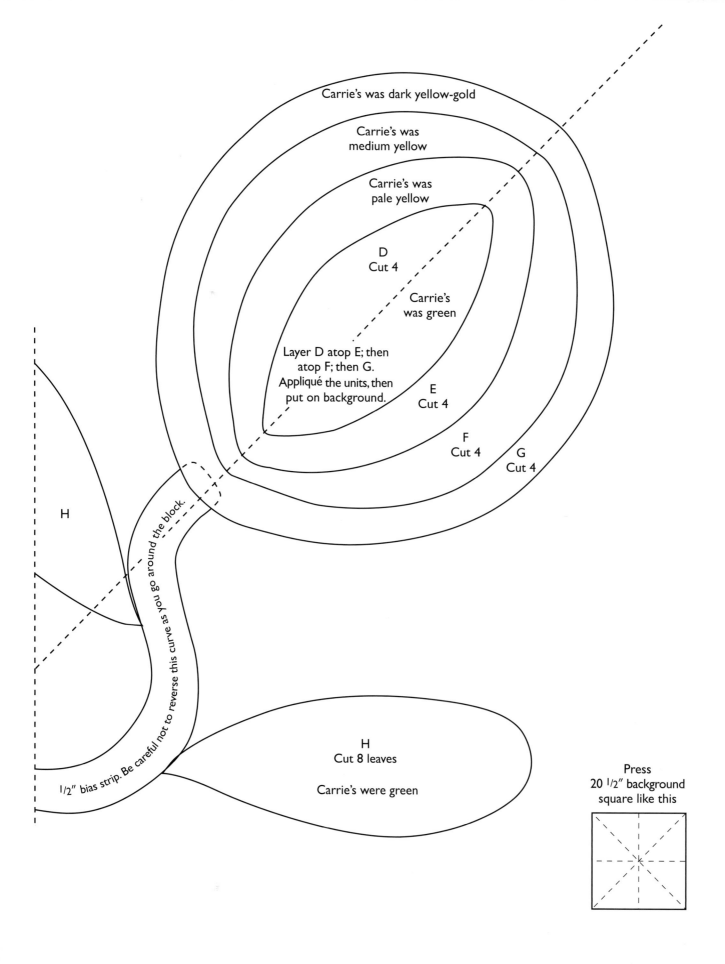

Carrie's was dark yellow-gold

Carrie's was
medium yellow

Carrie's was
pale yellow

D
Cut 4

Carrie's
was green

Layer D atop E; then
atop F; then G.
Appliqué the units, then
put on background.

E
Cut 4

F
Cut 4

G
Cut 4

H

1/2" bias strip. Be careful not to reverse this curve as you go around the block.

H
Cut 8 leaves

Carrie's were green

Press
20 1/2" background
square like this

Whig Rose

PATTERN 10 ✳ 15" X 25" FINISHED BLOCK

This quirky design that doesn't follow the formal symmetries of traditional appliqué has been adapted from an old design that Carrie Hall called Whig Rose (see page 115 of *Romance*). Several traditional patterns are named for the political party that thrived in the 1840s and early '50s. The name Whig comes to us from England. Today we hear a ring of pomposity but American Whigs viewed themselves as populists supporting a strong Congress in the face of autocratic Presidents, particularly Democrat Andrew Jackson.

HOW TO MAKE THIS BLOCK

Cut a rectangle of background fabric 15 1/2" x 25 1/2". Make up the rose by stitching the layers together and place it in the top right hand corner of the rectangle, about 2 1/2" down from the seam line and 1/2" to the right. Then lay the base (G) in the lower left hand corner, about 1/2" from the seams. Pin or glue a 1/2" bias strip (cut about 28" long) in a graceful curve for the major stem and trim and tuck under the flower and base. Make up the buds and lay them so they look balanced. Cut 2 strips of bias about 8" long each to make curved stems. Position the leaves last.

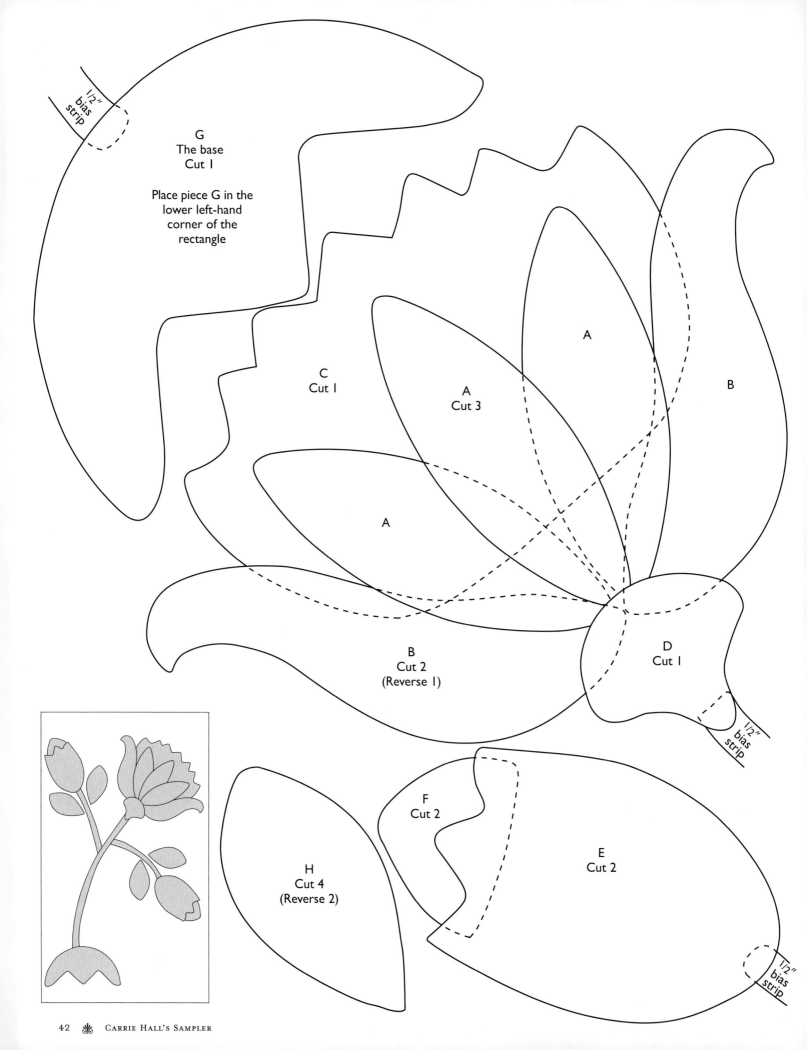

G
The base
Cut 1

Place piece G in the
lower left-hand
corner of the
rectangle

½" bias strip

C
Cut 1

A

A
Cut 3

B

A

B
Cut 2
(Reverse 1)

D
Cut 1

½" bias strip

H
Cut 4
(Reverse 2)

F
Cut 2

E
Cut 2

½" bias strip

Rose of Sharon

PATTERN II * 20" FINISHED BLOCK

Carrie drew this block from an antique quilt donated to the University of Kansas's art museum by Minnie Moodie, the museum's first curator, who called it Rose of Sharon, a metaphor from the King James version of the Bible. The original was made by Rena Coon Thomas of Sharon, Illinois (see page 183 in *Romance*). Carrie changed the buds a bit.

When this 20" block is finished, you are ready to set the last strip together and finish your top.

"I am the rose of Sharon, and the lily of the valleys." (Solomon 2:1)

HOW TO MAKE THIS BLOCK

This pattern is appliquéd onto a 20 1/2" square background. Follow the instructions on the patterns for cutting. Appliqué the rose (A+B) to the top left quadrant of the background as shown. Run a 3/4" strip of bias, about 17" long, to the bottom right hand corner. Find the triangle (F) that cuts through the rose on the pattern. Cut a triangle that size (do not add seams) and appliqué it over the stem and the right bottom corner. Appliqué each bud (B, D & E) as a unit and place in the top right hand corner and the bottom left hand corner. Using 1/2" bias strip, curve the stems as shown in the photo. Adjust the leaves to fit.

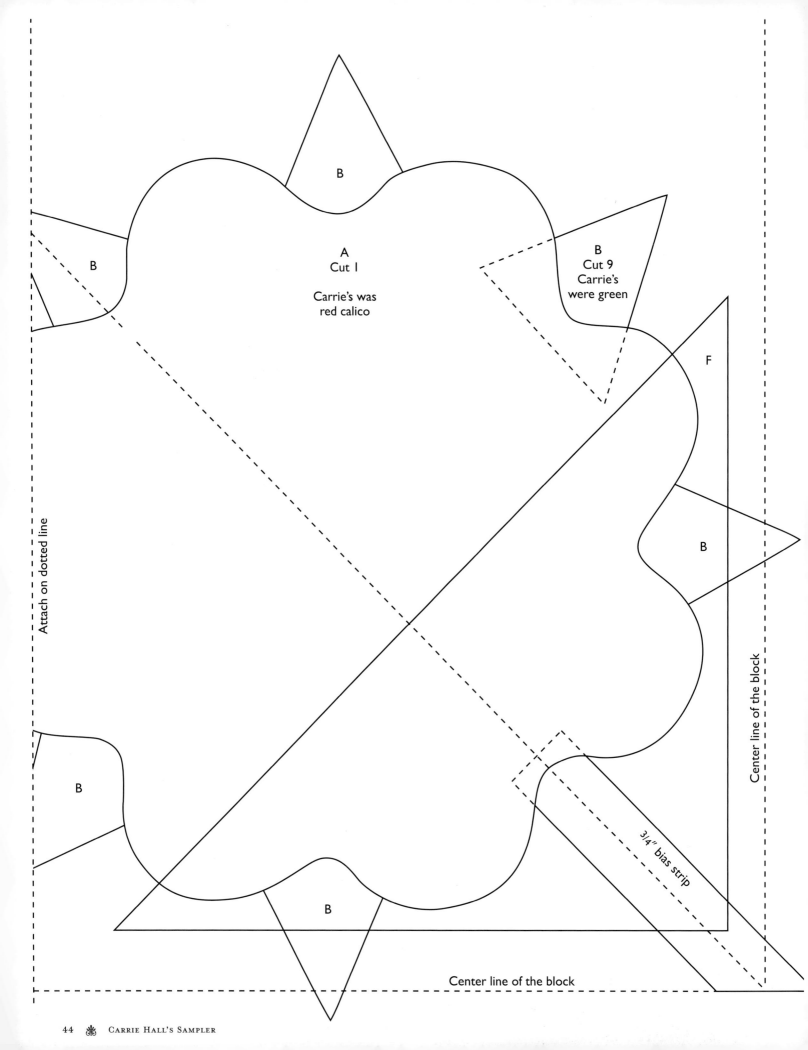

B

A
Cut I

Carrie's was
red calico

B
Cut 9
Carrie's
were green

B

F

B

Attach on dotted line

Center line of the block

B

3/4" bias strip

B

Center line of the block

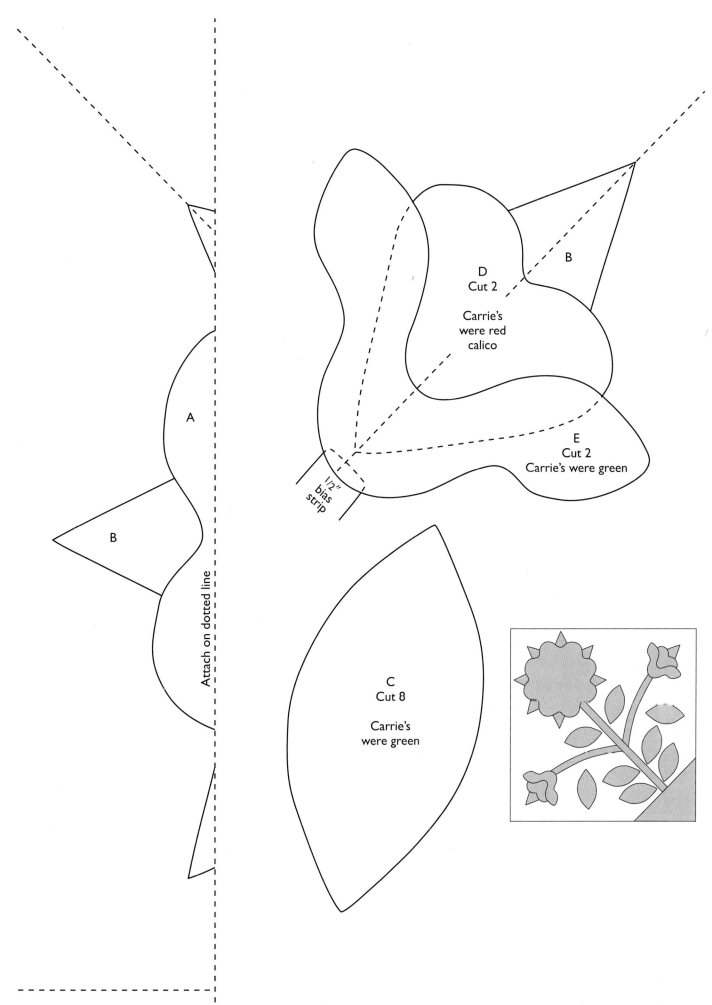

A

B

Attach on dotted line

D
Cut 2

Carrie's
were red
calico

B

E
Cut 2
Carrie's were green

1/2" bias strip

C
Cut 8

Carrie's
were green

Finishing

BORDER

One option for a pieced border is the adaptation of the Leavenworth Nine-Patch (see pattern 7, page 31).

ROTARY CUTTING
FOR EACH BLOCK, YOU NEED 2 1/8" SQUARES:

* 2 of background fabric
* 1 of a different light fabric
* 6 of dark fabric
* Make blocks and stitch together until your border size is reached.

The quilts pictured throughout the book show different options for finishing your border.

QUILTING

Echo quilt around each of the appliqué motifs and the center star by outlining the designs 3/4" apart. For the pieced border, quilt diagonal lines going one direction across the center of the nine patches. If you add the outer 5" plain border, quilt the cable there.

Diagonal line of border corner

Carrie Hall Sampler by Bettina Havig, Columbia, Missouri, 2000–2007. Bettina's handwork and fabric choices echo masterpiece quilts of the nineteenth century.

Carrie Hall's Sampler by Susannah Christenson, Lawrence, Kansas. 2001. Quilted by Lori Kukuk. Susannah designed her own appliquéd border.